To Julian.
Small is beautiful

A.E.B.

July 1981

VICTORIA
The Garden State

The skilful blending of colours is a feature of Ballarat's beautiful Botanic Gardens.

VICTORIA
THE GARDEN STATE

Kathrine Bell & Ian Wigney

Murray Child·Sydney

Page two:
Splashing fountains and a tranquil lake make a charming
setting for Melbourne's Exhibition Building in the inner city
suburb of Carlton.

Jacket illustrations (from top):
(a) Prince's Bridge and the Melbourne skyline from the Yarra
Bank; (b) The Queen Victoria Gardens, Melbourne;
(c) The P.S. Etona *moored at Echuca; (d) The stage coach*
at Sovereign Hill, Ballarat. (e) The rugged coastline in
the Port Campbell National Park;

Endpaper: Cradling and panning for gold.

First published 1979 by
Murray Child & Company
11 The Esplanade, Frenchs Forest, Australia, 2086
© Kathrine Bell and Ian Wigney, 1979
Designed and produced in Australia by the Publisher
Printed in Hong Kong by Bookprint
National Library of Australia Card Number and
ISBN 0 908048 10 6

Melbourne's skyline as seen from the Yarra Bank.

Victoria, the smallest State on the Australian mainland, occupies an area of less than 300,000 square kilometres, representing only 3 percent of the territory contained within the limits of this vast continent. South Australia lies beyond its western perimeter and in the north it is bounded by New South Wales, the actual border marked by the southern bank of the Murray River. In the State's northeastern section the border swings to the ocean at Cape Howe across rugged mountain country with a landscape scored by deep ravines and swiftly flowing rivers.

Victoria is a neat and compact State which is both scenically beautiful and widely diversified in all aspects of rural enterprise. It is an acknowledged leader in the fields of industrial and commercial development, with tourism playing an increasingly active role in the economy. With a higher concentration of population than the other States within the Commonwealth, its urban regions have, over the years, been undergoing a steady pattern of expansion, particularly those areas centred around the large industrial and commercial projects which have been established as decentralisation measures. The foundations of Victorian stability were laid long ago by harnessing its pastoral wealth, but the golden years that followed further guaranteed its durability and strength.

Victoria's capital city, Melbourne, is the second largest city in the Commonwealth of Australia. It is an important industrial and manufacturing centre and a busy port, with a population now tipping the three million mark. It was founded in 1835 by John Batman and John Pascoe Fawkner on the banks of the Yarra River, which winds through the city to its mouth in Hobson's Bay at the head of Port Phillip. Melbourne mixes modern charisma and liveliness with the elegance and grace of the 19th Century, its sleek high-rise structures blending harmoniously with the sturdy bluestone buildings of yesterday. Green lawns and shady trees fringe the Yarra Bank and many fine gardens have been interwoven into the urban pattern.

Melbourne's founders, Batman and 'Johnnie' Fawkner had little in common except a desire to settle in the Port Phillip district. Batman was a 'currency lad' who was born in Parramatta, NSW, in 1801. As a very young man he crossed to Tasmania where he acquired grazing land, but he was anxious to extend his pastoral holdings and Tasmania was too small. He cast covetous eyes towards the mainland, for he had heard about the prospects there from the Bass Strait sealers. Fawkner came from Launceston where he had kept an inn and published a newspaper. He was a small angry man who despised Batman and was determined to reach the mainland before him, but this

◄ *Sleek modern office blocks loom over Melbourne's dignified Collins Street.*

The famous Floral Clock in the Queen Victoria Gardens was presented to the city of Melbourne by the Watchmakers of Switzerland. Ten thousand plants are used to make up its face.

he did not succeed in doing. Batman's famous purchase of land from the Dutigalla tribe, which included the sites of Melbourne and Geelong, is well known to all Victorians, but it was a highly illegal transaction which caused trouble for Batman in later years. The Colonial Government had closed the Port Phillip district to settlement and refused to sanction his claim. Trouble erupted also between the rival founders and their respective parties over land rights which were still not resolved when Batman died in 1839.

Colonisation of the Port Phillip district was so rapid that officialdom in Sydney was forced to recognise its existence, and in 1837 Governor Bourke visited the settlement. He named it Melbourne after Lord Melbourne, the then Prime Minister of Britain, and delegated surveyor Robert Hoddle to draw up a town plan. Hoddle selected the grid system which gave Melbourne the wide straight streets that distinguishes it from other less fortunate cities.

Because the colonists of Port Phillip were free, many of them having followed the original founders from Tasmania, and wished to shape their own future without interference, they were soon pressing for separation from New South Wales. This was officially proclaimed in July 1851, only a few days before the news of the first Victorian gold strike reached Melbourne. This was the prelude to a gold rush which would sweep across the Colony like a forest fire, bringing shiploads of immigrants from overseas, and transforming placid, provincial Melbourne into a riproaring frontier town.

As conditions settled the unsavoury image gradually disappeared and Melbourne developed into a centre of culture and refinement. Grand public buildings sprang up and the elegant homes of the *nouveau-riche* appeared in the spreading suburbs. The National Trust of Victoria has been very active in acquiring and restoring several of the old mansions that still survive. *Como* in South Yarra and *Rippon Lea* in Elsternwick are examples of their excellent work.

Many of the old-style buildings have, in the name of progress, fallen victims of the demolisher's hammer to make way for modern apartment buildings and office blocks. Collins Street has suffered greatly in this way. The citizens of Melbourne, concerned that their heritage was being threatened, stood firm

Fountains play in Melbourne's Civic Square. Concerts are held regularly in the Town Hall which stands nearby.

Tasma Terrace, a rare group of three-storey terrace houses in Parliament Place, which is now the headquarters of the National Trust of Victoria. The iron lace on the balconies and verandahs is typical of the late 19th Century.

The cool green tranquillity of the Queen Victoria Gardens is welcome on a warm summer day.

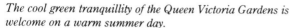

Como *in South Yarra represents the grace and dignity of an earlier era. It was purchased from John Brown, a master builder, by Charles Henry Armytage in 1864 and is now the property of the National Trust.*

A waterfall and lake are among the interesting features of the Rippon Lea gardens. This elegant mansion in Elsternwick was given to the National Trust by its last owner, Mrs Louisa Jones.

One of Melbourne's famous landmarks is Captain Cook's Cottage in the Fitzroy Gardens. It was brought from Yorkshire in England and erected here in 1934, Victoria's centenary year.

Puffing Billy, the veteran Edwardian train, is a familiar sight as it winds through the Dandenong Ranges. It has been carefully restored by the Puffing Billy Preservation Society.

Magnificent panoramas of the surrounding countryside can be seen from vantage points in the Dandenong Ranges. ▶

and now sufficient numbers of buildings have been spared to preserve the atmosphere of gracious living for which the city is famed.

Although most of the rural land on Melbourne's outer fringe has been engulfed in the relentless encroachment of the suburban sprawl, it has not yet noticeably affected the sequestered charm of the Dandenong Ranges which rim the city's eastern limits. This is a magical world of cool green gullies, forests and tree-ferns, birds and colourful gardens. Boarding the veteran train, Puffing Billy, at Belgrave and winding through the mountains to Emerald Lake is a unique experience for visitors, for it is the same route taken by the pioneers who settled in the Dandenongs during Edwardian times.

The Yarra River rises among the high ridges of the Great Dividing Range, and as it spills down the valley on its way to Melbourne and the sea, it passes through a landscape which is touched with grandeur. Towns such as Healesville on the Watts River, a tributary of the Yarra and famous for the Sir Colin MacKenzie Sanctuary for Australian wildlife, Warburton

nestling cosily in the mountains, and Marysville near the ski slopes of Lake Mountain present a picture of tranquillity and charm.

The You Yang Mountains frame the flat lands of the Werribee Plains which stretch in a wide sweeping arc between Melbourne and Geelong which, standing on the shores of Corio Bay, a large identation of the Western shoreline of Port Phillip, is Victoria's largest provincial city and second largest port.

Geelong's site was chosen in 1838 by Robert Hoddle and the ground plan was laid out later that year by Henry Smyth. The first settlers to take up land in the Geelong district were J.A. Cowrie and David Stead who shipped their stock from Van Diemen's Land to the pastures surrounding Corio Bay in 1835. They were followed in 1837 by Dr Alexander Thomson who was elected Mayor in 1891 after Geelong was proclaimed a city. Captain Foster Fyans was appointed Police Magistrate in 1837 and built a small cottage on the Moorabool River near its confluence with the Barwon.

Although Geelong was a commonly used port of entry for the

Ballarat gold fields it was not until 1893 when a rock-bar was dredged from the entrance to Corio Bay that it reached its full potential as a port. These days it has facilities for the handling of about 9,000,000 tonnes of cargo each year. Geelong has an important place in Victoria's industrial network with an enviable reputation for the manufacture of high quality textiles, particularly woollen cloth. It is also the centre of an active rural scene with the surrounding pastures supporting large numbers of sheep and dairy cattle.

South of Geelong the shoreline of Port Phillip swings eastward to form a neck of land known as the Bellarine Peninsula. The popular holiday resorts of Portarlington, Indented Head — John Batman's first landfall in Port Phillip — St Leonards and Queenscliff lie scattered along the foreshores of the bay. At the head of the peninsula, Point Lonsdale faces Point Nepean across the reef-strewn waters of the Rip, Port Phillip's narrow and dangerous entrance. Two of Victoria's finest surfing beaches are to found fronting Bass Strait at Ocean Grove and Barwon Heads on the southern side of the Bellarine Peninsula.

The Barwon River which rises in the Otway Ranges winds down through the mountains, passes through Geelong and the Connewarre Lakes to its outlet into Bass Strait at Barwon Heads. Early in the century an attempt was made to navigate ships up the Barwon to Geelong, but heavy seas and a rock shelf at the river's mouth prevented reasonable access and the scheme was abandoned.

The dramatic beauty of Victoria's southern coast is revealed in all its majesty from the sweeping contours of the Great Ocean Road which clings to the foothills of the rugged Otway Range. At times the road rises high above the rocky coast, then drops suddenly down to sea level to wind around the wide sandy beaches that fringe the shore. A scatter of holiday resorts, Anglesea, Lorne, Wye River, Apollo Bay and several others nestle in the shadow of the ranges which loom above the coastline.

The Otways, with their stately forests and avenues of luxuriant tree-ferns are believed to be the remains of the ancient land bridge linking the Australian mainland with Tasmania. The Great Ocean Road was constructed by returned servicemen of World War 1 in memory of the great deeds performed by them in battle. Opened to travellers in 1932, it covers a distance of 320 km from Torquay to Peterborough. In spite of its spectacular beauty, this is a savage coast with a sinister reputation as a graveyard for ships. Many fine vessels

▲
The popular surfing beach at Ocean Grove on the southern side of the Bellarine Peninsula.

Point Nepean at the tip of the Mornington Peninsula is washed by the Rip, Port Phillip's narrow entrance.

◄
Sunlight and shadow in the gardens at Geelong, Victoria's largest provincial city.

Loch Ard Gorge in the Port Campbell National Park was the scene of a tragic shipwreck in June 1878. ►

A panoramic view of the spectacular Bay of Martyrs in the Port Campbell National Park. The Great Ocean Road winds past the rugged coastline from Torquay to Peterborough.

A peaceful anchorage at Port Fairy on Victoria's south-western coast. ➤

London Bridge, a rock formation sculptured by wind and tide near Port Campbell.

have been smashed on the jagged reefs during the wild storms of winter.

One of the worst disasters occurred in June 1878, when the *Loch Ard* broke up on the rocks of Mutton Bird Island, a treacherous outcrop just beyond Loch Ard Gorge. The two survivors, a young seaman and a girl passenger, were washed into the Gorge and found shelter in a cave until help arrived. Several bodies were recovered from the sea and were buried in a small graveyard on the top of the cliffs. This lonely spot is now enclosed within the limits of the Port Campbell National Park which is renowned for its magnificent scenery, and has become a favourite stopping place for travellers on the Great Ocean Road.

At Peterborough the coast and the Great Ocean Road are left behind. The road swings inland and winds through lush grazing land before joining the Princes Highway near the large and prosperous coastal city of Warrnambool, an important centre in Victoria's south-western district. There is an excellent surfing beach at Warrnambool, sheltered rock pools for the more timid swimmers, horse racing, fishing and scenery to suit all tastes. An interesting Maritime Museum has been established on Flagstaff Hill and contains many reminders of the early ships and the hazards they faced.

The historic fishing township of Port Fairy, a few kilometres further on, was named by a sea-captain, James Wishart after his ship the *Fairy* when he took shelter from a violent storm in the mouth of the Moyne River in 1810. Port Fairy was closely associated with the sealing trade in the early days, and when the seals disappeared it became a well-known whaling station. Its first settlers, Charles Mills and his brother John, used it as a base for their operations before they retired from the whaling business. Charles later took up farming, but John, still feeling the call of the sea, joined the coastal shipping trade. Both their homes still exist, in company with several others that have been classified by the National Trust.

In 1835, when the Batman-Fawkner colony was founded on the banks of the Yarra River, the first permanent settlement in Victoria, at Portland Bay in the far south-west of the Colony had been in existence for almost a year. In November 1834, Edward Henty and his party disembarked from the *Thistle* and immediately commenced building huts and ploughing the land for planting crops.

Portland, as well as Port Fairy, has close ties with both the sealing and whaling industries. Captain William Dutton, who was involved with both these lucrative enterprises, visited Portland regularly before the Hentys came and later settled permanently in a cottage overlooking the bay. He is buried in the old cemetery at Narrawong.

Edward Henty was a member of a wealthy and influential grazing family who had immigrated from Britain to the Swan River Colony in Western Australia in 1829, and from there moved across to Van Diemen's Land. As they were anxious to expand their pastoral holdings to the mainland, and ignoring the Government ruling that settlement in the Port Phillip district was illegal, they selected Portland Bay as being the most suitable place to establish themselves. They were followed by others equally determined on expansion.

Today, Portland, named after the Duke of Portland by Lieutenant James Grant as he sailed past in the *Lady Nelson* in December 1800, is a picturesque and progressive town on the shores of a crescent-shaped bay. Its port facilities have been considerably extended over the years to allow for the increase in wheat exports, and a large complex for the storage of wool has been built on the outskirts of the town. Portland's grand old colonial buildings are the tangible link between the pioneer past and the present. At least two of them, the Customs House and Edward Henty's home, *Burswood,* rate an 'A' classification by the National Trust.

The coastline beyond Portland is a spectacular procession of beaches, great misty headlands and sand dunes that curve away beyond the horizon to the South Australian border. The hinterland is soft and green, reflecting the rural richness which lured the pioneers to these shores in the footsteps of the Hentys. The coastal plain is rimmed by the massive bulk of the Grampians mountain range which was discovered and named by Major Thomas Mitchell in 1836. The forests that mantle the

The Flagstaff Hill Maritime Museum at Warrnambool.

The foundation stone of St John's Presbyterian Church, Warrnambool, was laid on 17th September 1874.

The trim landscaped gardens in the busy coastal city of Warrnambool.

This large cauldron was used for boiling down whale blubber during the whaling days at Portland. It now stands on the shore overlooking the bay.

17

Beautiful Bridgewater Bay near Portland was the scene of many shipwrecks over the years.

The Customs House in Portland has been classified 'A' by the National Trust. It was built in 1850.

Cloud shadows pattern the coastline at Discovery Bay which sweeps westward into South Australia. ➤

▲ *Portland's colourful Botanic Gardens were laid out in 1857.
The curator's cottage has been restored and furnished in the
fashion of 100 years ago.*

▼*The rugged peaks of the Grampians outlined against the sky.*

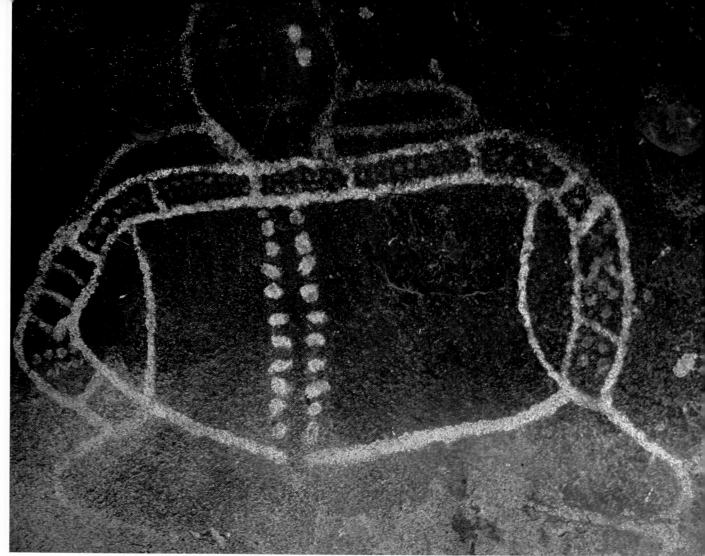

▲ *Bunjil, a Dreamtime ancestor of the aboriginal people of south-eastern Australia, is depicted in a rocky cavern in the Black Range about 11 km from Stawell.*

▼ *An interesting exhibit at Stawell's Mini World which traces the development of man and his varying life-styles by means of models and commentaries. Photo: Chris Wigney.*

Grampians cover an area of more than 210,000 hectares, and are controlled by the Victorian Forest Commission. Walking tracks and access roads have been provided for the benefit of visitors wishing to explore the rugged terrain.

The Grampians abound in rare fauna and flora, and from late winter to early summer the hillsides are ablaze with wild flowers. There are certain places throughout the mountains which were sacred to the aboriginal people who lived in this part of Victoria and who have left behind them samples of their rare artistic skill in the form of rock paintings.

Nestling in the foothills of the Grampians, Stawell is the centre of a district which includes the township of Great Western which is a noted producer of high quality wines. Stawell is also surrounded by excellent sheep-raising country, and the North-Western Woollen Mills which were opened in 1923 produce particularly fine woollen material including blankets and furnishing fabrics. The mills were originally established to provide jobs for a town in danger of dying after the closure of the gold mines in 1916.

Gold had been discovered at Stawell in 1853 and the first strike was soon followed by other finds of both alluvial and reef gold. The alluvial finds were short-lived, but the rich quartz reefs were worked for 60 years. The famous foot-race, the Stawell Gift, which is run during the three-day Easter Athletic Carnival, is a legacy from a group of successful ex-miners who had gone into business in the town. In 1878, they formed the Athletic Club and inaugurated the first Gift race which had prize money to the value of 20 sovereigns. Today, athletes come from across the Commonwealth and from overseas to compete.

The Stawell gold rush was one of many that took place in Victoria during the eventful 1850s. They had a profound effect on the agrarian economy which had evolved since the foundation of the Colony in 1834. The immigrants who poured into the country from all parts of the world brought with them fresh ideals and concepts from a world fraught with change, and this naturally made an impact on the colonial society of which they had become a part. In the melting pot of the diggings, unity and comradeship were born. This kindled the first faint spark of nationalism which was to flame into the Federation movement as the century drew to its close.

Underlying the harsh, crowded conditions on the gold fields was a simmering undercurrent of resentment over the hated miners licences which had been introduced by the Government as a revenue booster and to control prospecting. At the prohibitive cost of 30/- a month they were beyond the means of many miners, and digging without a licence, or with one that had expired, warranted a penalty that was unnecessarily harsh. On the Ballarat fields the discontent erupted into open rebellion at the Eureka Stockade, when, on 3rd December, 1854, 200 miners, armed and angry and flying their own flag emblazoned with the Southern Cross faced the Government troopers sent in haste by Governor Hotham.

After a brief exchange, the rebels were quickly defeated by the trained troops. They were arrested and were later tried for treason, but the weight of the public opinion forced an acquittal for them all. The licences were abolished in favour of the more

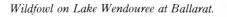
Wildfowl on Lake Wendouree at Ballarat.

Panning for gold at Sovereign Hill, the reconstructed mining town at Ballarat.

A fine display of begonias in the conservatory at the Ballarat Botanic Gardens.

▲ *The monument commemorating the Eureka Stockade at Ballarat.*

▼*Vintage tram at Ballarat.*

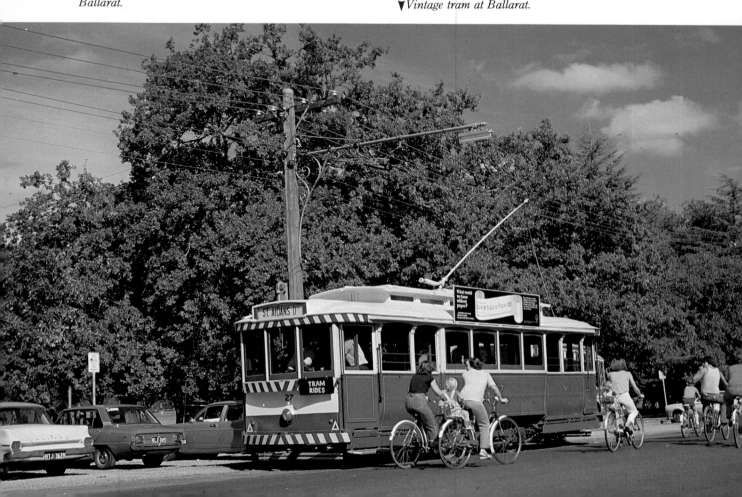

*Kryal Castle at Ballarat is packed with reminders of the
medieval days. It is one of the city's most fascinating
tourist attractions.*

realistic and much less expensive Miner's Right. By showing a
united front, the Ballarat diggers had made their point and
justice was done.

The Ballarat goldfields were discovered in August 1851 and
were mined successfully until 1918. Progress was made from
the surface alluvial deposits to the deeper alluvial leads, and
from there to the reefs of gold-bearing quartz which were
hidden deeply beneath the ground. It was an exceptionally rich
field yielding a high percentage of nuggets which varied greatly
in size. The largest one found, the Welcome, was unearthed by
two Cornish miners in 1858 and weighed more than 60 kilo-
grams. After being exhibited in Australia and overseas, it was
finally converted into sovereigns by the Royal Mint.

The foundations of Ballarat's imposing public buildings are
firmly entwined with the city's golden roots, and the prosperity
that launched them also provided the means for establishing the
artistically landscaped Botanic Gardens which fringe the shores
of Lake Wendouree. In late summer and early autumn the
masses of begonias which are Ballarat's pride are displayed in
their full glory. The Begonia Festival attracts visitors from all
parts of the Commonwealth.

The rattling gold escorts have gone now. Vanished, too, are
the ragged lines of hopeful seekers who trudged from
Melbourne and Geelong along the rutted road which has been
replaced by a modern highway. The mines and their associated
paraphernalia have long since disappeared, but Ballarat still
remembers. Sovereign Hill, an area of wasteland pitted with
abandoned mines, presents Ballarat as it used to be. Since it
was opened in November 1970, thousands of visitors have been
able to see for themselves how it was in those tumultuous days.

Bendigo, where gold was also found in 1851, lies between the
Campaspe and Lodden Rivers in Central Victoria. Like Ballarat
before the rush began, it was a quiet grazing district, situated
on part of a large sheep property called Bendigo's Run. Alluvial
gold first attracted the prospectors to the Bendigo fields, but
the discovery of the valley's rich quartz reefs, particularly in the
Victoria Hill area, brought thousands more to try their luck. It
has been roughly estimated that on today's values about
$15,000,000 worth of gold was taken from the Victoria Hill
fields alone. The Bendigo gold fields were worked continuously
for more than 100 years, and the last operating mine, the
Central Deborah, closed in 1954. This has been developed as
tourist attraction.

The Chinese were familiar figures on all the Victorian gold
fields. The majority of them were employed by wealthy
Chinese businessmen who had financed their venture and to
whom they were bound until their contracts expired. They
were quiet and industrious, and caused little trouble, but they

were the unwitting focus of several unpleasant incidents prompted in the main by jealousy. Some returned to their homeland when they had repaid their sponsors, but others remained in Victoria. The descendants of those who worked on the Bendigo fields are now deeply involved with the city's affairs. They enliven the Easter Fair each year with their splendid Sun Loong Dragon. The Chinese Joss House at Emu Point is a sample of the rich cultural and religious heritage they brought with them and is the only one of the four built in the area that still survives. It has been classified and restored by the National Trust.

Bendigo's premier tourist attraction is the Pottery which was established in 1857 by George Duncan Guthrie, a potter turned gold miner who discovered the clay suited to his craft while searching for gold. After surviving a period of decline the Bendigo Pottery has been revitalised and now produces a wide range of high quality work, which is much admired and sought after by visitors.

There are relics and reminders of the golden years right through Victoria's central district. Maldon, 37 km from Bendigo, has been classified as First Notable Town in Australia by the National Trust for its assembly of historic buildings which date from the days when it was a thriving gold town. Nearby Castlemaine once rivalled Melbourne in size and population when great quantities of alluvial gold were found throughout the district. As the gold ran out and the population started to drift away, the concerned citizens directed their skills into other enterprises and so prevented the town from falling into decay.

The most outstanding building in Castlemaine is the elegant old Market which was built in 1862 and has a graceful pillared facade reminiscent of the Classical period in architecture. As the need for a market in Castlemaine diminished, the old building fell into a bad state of repair, and as it appeared to be unsafe, was threatened with demolition. It was then acquired by the National Trust who undertook its restoration. This was completed in 1974, and it now houses an interesting district museum.

The countryside which surrounds these interesting and historic areas is scenically attractive and supports a wide range of rural activities. After the gold disappeared, many of the miners settled in the region and concentrated on farming, and this played an important part in the development of this district and others throughout Victoria.

The effects of the gold discoveries had a bearing though indirectly, on the development of the settlements along the Murray River. This was particularly true of Echuca, which was near the Bendigo diggings, and situated at the point on the river which is closest to Melbourne, was a natural choice for

◄ *The Post Office at Bendigo is the largest outside Melbourne. It was built in 1887 and has been classified by the National Trust.*

▲ *The main altar in the Chinese Joss House at Bendigo.*

The Stables Gallery at the Bendigo Pottery which was established in 1857. The pottery is displayed in this old building, which dates from 1880.

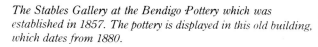

▲ *The elegant Shamrock Hotel in Bendigo contains 100 rooms*
and has been classified by the National Trust.

► *The colourful gardens in the town of Castlemaine, an old gold*
mining centre 42 km from Bendigo.

▲ *The main street of Maldon which has been classified*
First Notable Town in Australia by the National Trust.

Wheat harvesting in central Victoria. Grain crops are also ➤
grown extensively in the Wimmera district.

▼ *Lake Eppalock on the Campaspe River irrigates northern*
Victoria and also supplements Bendigo's water supply. It was
commenced in June 1960 and completed in April 1964
by the State Rivers and Water Supply Commission of Victoria.

An interior view of the Castlemaine Market which was opened▼
in 1862. It has been restored by the National Trust and
now houses a district museum.

The underground bar of the Star Hotel in Echuca. The Star was built in 1867 and was one of the many hotels existing in Echuca when the river trade was in its heyday. It now houses the Port Information Centre.

Echuca Wharf was built in 1865 and has now been restored together with other buildings of historical interest by the Port of Echuca Restoration Project. ➤

a crossing. In 1846, James Maiden, the founder of the New South Wales town of Moama, commenced operating a punt from the northern bank of the river to enable the inland graziers to transport their stock to the Melbourne markets. In 1853, Henry Hopwood, an enterprising businessman and an ex-convict from Tasmania, established himself on the southern bank. He set up a larger punt and a pontoon bridge across the Murray and also operated a punt across the Campaspe River in opposition to Maiden. This spot soon came to be known as Hopwood's Ferry and was the nucleus of the city of Echuca.

In the same year William Randell in the paddle steamer *Mary Ann* and Francis Cadell in the *Lady Augusta* raced each other upstream from Goolwa near the Murray mouth, past Swan Hill to Gannawarra where Randell overtook Cadell and steamed on to Moama where he was given a hero's welcome. This proved without a doubt that the Murray was navigable and ushered in the steam boat era which, for more than 50 years, brought cargoes of wool from the distant inland stations to the railhead at Echuca. Not only did the steamers carry goods and passengers, but they brought news of the doings in the outside world to the isolated settlements and properties fringing the river and its tributaries.

Echuca was, during the heyday of the paddle-wheelers, the largest inland port in Australia, but as the network of railways spread throughout the country, the need for the slower form of tranport declined. The steamers became redundant and one by one they disappeared. However, the sharp increase in tourism along the Murray River stimulated wide interest in the romantic days of the steamers and those that still survived were brought out of retirement to be restored and rejuvenated. Some of them now serve as museums, others such as the *Rothbury* and the *Pyap* were absorbed into the tourist cruise fleet to once again ride the river. The largest and the grandest of them all was the *Gem* which was built in Moama in 1876 and now rests on a small lake at the entrance to the Swan Hill Pioneer Settlement. It houses a restaurant, the Settlement's office and a small art gallery.

The old section of Echuca which fronts the riverbank is closely associated with the paddle-steamer days, and in 1969 was declared an Historic Area by the National Trust. In an effort to preserve its antique character the ambitious Port of Echuca Restoration Project scheme was initiated. Work commenced in 1973 and although it is still proceeding a great deal has already been done. Visitors can now wander through the old port and its surroundings and see how it looked during the years from 1870 to 1885 when the river boat trade was at its peak. The restored paddle-steamer *Pevensey* is moored at the wharf and it is intended, as a further touch of authenticity, that she will pull the heavily laden barge *Ada* around the loop of the river opposite the wharf. The *Adelaide,* which was built at Echuca in 1866, presently rests in Henry Hopwood Park near the river, but it is hoped that she will one day be refloated.

In 1836, Major Thomas Mitchell who camped on the site where the city of Swan Hill now stands named the spot after the numbers of swans who disturbed his slumbers with their noisy cries. The first settlers in the district were the Beveridge brothers who travelled with their stock from Kilmore in the Port Phillip district in 1846 and built a small

The paddle-steamer Gem *serves as the entrance to the Swan Hill Pioneer Settlement. It was built at Moama in 1876.*

The Post Office and the barber's shop at the Swan Hill Pioneer Settlement, which is a re-creation of the lifestyle of the settlers during the latter half of the 19th Century.

The paddle-steamer Rothbury *entering Lock 11 at Mildura.*

Sailing craft preparing to launch at Lake Boga which is one of a string of lakes and lagoons along the flood plain of the Lodden River, a tributary of the Murray.

These Dethridge meters are a common sight in irrigation areas. They register the amount of water used by each property owner.

Rio Vista *at Mildura was once the home of W. B. Chaffey, who, with his brother George, pioneered irrigation in the Sunraysia district of Victoria. It now houses the Mildura Art Gallery and a museum.*

homestead which they named *Tyntyndyer,* an aboriginal word meaning 'song of birds'. As the years passed extensions were made to the original house, and in 1876 it was sold to the Holloway family whose descendants are still in possession.

The city of Swan Hill has paid an impressive tribute to the pioneers by developing the Pioneer Settlement which re-creates along the banks of the river a small bush township of the 19th Century, complete with craftsmen and shopkeepers performing their daily tasks. Visitors who come to explore find it a most enjoyable and informative experience.

Although the river is no longer used as a means of transport, it has, with the introduction of irrigation, gained a new and vital significance. Sleek dairy herds graze on the lush pastures and fodder crops, vineyards and orchards enfold the landscape in a mantle of green.

In 1886, Alfred Deakin, a Victorian Member of Parliament and destined to become a future Prime Minister of Australia engaged the services of the Chaffey brothers who had pioneered a successful irrigation scheme in California. Their expertise laid the foundations of the prosperous Sunraysia district which is one of the most productive areas in Victoria. Until the Chaffeys irrigation scheme was inaugurated, this region was a wilderness of windswept red sand, and since before 1846 had been part of a large and arid cattle run. Today, it is a tapestry interwoven with citrus groves and vineyards surrounding the sunny city of Mildura which has become in recent years a popular wintering place for residents of the colder climates.

With its abundant rainfall, Victoria does not have the areas of desert country which are found throughout its neighbouring States. An exception is the region which lies to the south-west of Mildura and stretches on to the South Australian border. This is the Mallee country, a land of stunted vegetation, mostly eucalypts, wide horizons and a surprising variety of natural flora and fauna. In order to preserve the unique character of this semi-arid land and to protect the indigenous animal and plant life, three National Parks, Wyperfeld, Little Desert and Hattah Lakes, have been established.

At one time the undulating wheat lands of the Wimmera were also covered with thick mallee scrub, but the pioneers cleared it with their primitive implements, and planting wheat, so transformed it into the granary of Victoria. At harvest time the sea of grain stretches in a golden carpet to the far horizon. At the heart of this rich district, the city of Horsham, 317 km south of Mildura, is the important commercial centre.

The Murray-Darling river system is the largest in Australia and drains an area of 1,036,000 square kilometres in a network of tributaries stretching from Queensland and north-western New South Wales to northern Victoria and part of South Australia. From its source in the ranges that straddle the Victoria-New South Wales border to its outlet to the Southern Ocean at Encounter Bay in South Australia, the Murray covers a distance of 2,500 km. Swollen by the melting snows of spring and fed by its swiftly flowing mountain tributaries it tumbles from the mountains through deep gorges and across high green valleys where cattle graze to emerge from the foothills and immediately plunge into the Hume Lake. This huge storage dam conserves the waters of the Murray as well as these of its tributary the Mitta Mitta. It thunders over

Loading cattle at Horsham in the Wimmera.

Sheep grazing on the banks of the Murray River near Albury-Wodonga.

The Beechworth Powder Magazine on the outskirts of the town was built in 1858 during the gold rush days.

This pump was designed by George Chaffey and saw service from 1889 until 1955. It stands in a small park opposite Rio Vista.

Weathered rocks in Beechworth Gorge. Ned Kelly, the bushranger, was imprisoned in Beechworth gaol on two occasions.

After leaving Lake Mulwala the Murray River thunders through the Yarrawonga Weir.

46

The tranquil lake at Beechworth.

Ladies' Day at Benalla Bowling Club.

▶ *The town of Mt Beauty nestles at the foot of Mt Bogong, near the High Plains and the ski resort of Falls Creek. An $80 million dollar hydro-electricity scheme has been established here by the State Electricity Commission of Victoria.*

A pretty scene in the gardens at Benalla which is a progressive city in the Goulburn Valley.

the Hume Weir then sweeps onward to the twin cities of Albury (in New South Wales) and Wodonga (in Victoria) which stand on either side of the old river crossing used by the pioneers. The Union Bridge now spans the Murray's widening stream.

Albury occupies a portion of what was once Mungabareena Station which was owned by C.H. Ebden, and Wodonga was the name given by the Huon brothers to their large property on the river's southern bank. Hume and Hovell passed this way in 1824. They were the first explorers to sight the Murray, but after naming it the Hume they hurried on towards the coast and Port Phillip Bay. It was Sturt, in 1830, who named the 'broad and noble river' Murray in honour of Sir George Murray who was at that time Secretary of State for the Colonies. The aboriginal people who had camped and hunted along its banks since the legendary Dreamtime knew it as Millewa.

In 1836, Major Mitchell, while on his famous Australia Felix journey through the interior of Victoria, proved what Sturt had suspected, that the Hume and the Murray were one and the same. The small serene townships of Beechworth, Yackandandah, Rutherglen and Chiltern which lie on the periphery of the river were once bustling gold towns. Nowadays Rutherglen is famed for its high quality wines. The Australian novelist Henry Handel Richardson who wrote the trilogy, *The Fortunes of Richard Mahony* spent her childhood at Chiltern which is also vineyard country. The Kelly Gang whose exploits are woven into the fabric of Australian folklore once wandered through the mountains rimming the Ovens and Goulburn Valleys, sweeping down from the ranges to raid the nearby towns. Tiny Glenrowan was the scene, in June 1880, of Ned Kelly's last shoot-out with the police. He was captured, convicted on a murder charge and hanged in the Old Melbourne Gaol in November of the same year.

The Ovens and Goulburn Rivers, which are both tributaries of the Murray, flow through a landscape which is both richly productive and scenically beautiful. Dairy farms and vineyards nestle beside orchards which supply large quantities of fruit to the canning factories at Shepparton. In recent years, tourism has become an important facet of the district's economy. The well-known Victorian ski resorts of Mt Buller, Mt Hotham, Mt Buffalo and Falls Creek are to be found in the heights of the Great Dividing Range where both the Ovens and Goulburn Rivers rise. Summer also attracts visitors, including fishermen and water sports enthusiasts who enjoy exploring the tranquil lakes and streams that thread their way through the rugged high country.

The mountain tiers stretch onward to the southern horizon, thrust upward to Victoria's central spine then drop away to form the high plateau of Gippsland where lakes and ocean mingle in a symphony of blue. In 1839, Angus McMillan crossed these wind-swept uplands searching for drought-free land for pasturing the stock belonging to his employer Lachlan McAlister. He established Numbla-Munjie Station, now Ensay, and the following year continued his explorations, this time discovering the Gippsland Lakes and reaching the coast at Port Albert. He was so impressed with the new land that he called it Caledonia Australis, but the Polish explorer Strzelecki, who followed closely in his tracks, renamed it Gippsland in honour of

The popular ski slopes at Falls Creek.

▶ *A peaceful scene at Bright, on the Ovens River. It is located near the popular snow fields at Mt Hotham, Mt Buffalo and Falls Creek.*

Beautiful Lake Eildon is located high in the mountains near the headwaters of the Goulburn River, and irrigates a large area of Northern Victoria. It is also a most favoured venue for water sports.

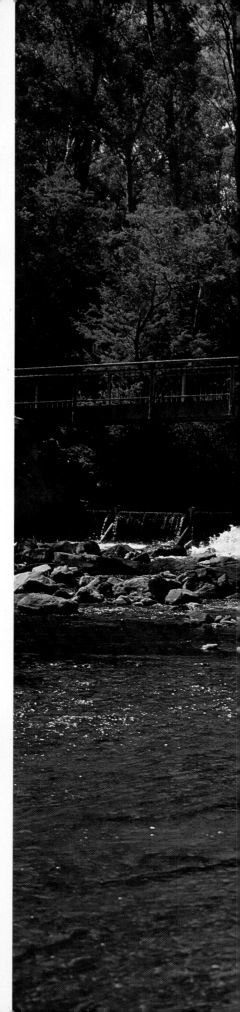

*The winery at Chateau Tahbilk in the Goulburn Valley
was established in 1860. It has received more than 300 awards
for the high quality wines produced from its vineyards
over the years.*

► *Major Mitchell camped in this secluded spot on the Goulburn
River on 8th October, 1836.*

*Grape picking at the Mitchelton vineyards. This winery was
was established in 1969. Major Thomas Mitchell crossed the
Goulburn River at this spot in 1836.*

the Governor of New South Wales, Sir George Gipps. The excellent grazing prospects as described by the explorers invited settlement, and a seaport established at Port Albert was used as a port of entry by incoming settlers and as an export outlet for their produce.

Because its mountainous terrain coupled with regions of almost impenetrable forest presented major problems for the road builders, Gippsland was, for many years, accessible only by sea. It was not until the railway was extended to Sale in 1878 that the Gippsland settlers had a direct land route to Melbourne. Many years were to elapse before a complete network of road and rail links was developed. From 1855, the Gippsland Lakes were widely used as a means of transport, but with the natural entrance surrounded by shifting shoals and sandbars, it presented a danger to shipping. A plan was devised to carve a new channel through the narrow strip of land separating the lakes from the ocean. This man-made entrance was situated near Cunninghame, now Lakes Entrance, and was completed in 1889. The problem of access had been solved, but the increased salinity of the lakes caused by the inrush of sea-water has had a detrimental effect on the ecology of the area.

Lakes Entrance is now a lively and popular resort town which offers a variety of activities for the holiday-maker. There is excellent surfing on the long wide stretches of Ninety Mile Beach, safe swimming along the lake shores and many opportunities for fishing and cruising along the winding waterways. Lakes Entrance is also the home port for the largest commercial fishing fleet in Victoria.

Gippsland's scenery is a study in contrasts, embracing the cool stillness of the mountains, the undulating rural countryside of the coastal hinterland, and an indented shoreline which stretches from Cape Howe in the north to the surf-scarred cliffs of Wilson's Promontory, the most southerly point on the Australian mainland. Point Hicks, on the coast of Gippsland, was the first landfall made by Captain Cook on his voyage up the continent's eastern coast in 1770. This historic spot is now enclosed by the Captain James Cook National Park.

Gippsland is well-endowed with natural resources. Its forests provide timber for building and for paper manufacture, gold was found throughout the district in the early days, and the massive deposits of brown coal, the remains of vast prehistoric forests, provide fuel for the power stations of the Latrobe Valley which supply most of Victoria's electricity needs. But most vital of all to the Australian economy are the giant oil rigs which are located in Bass Strait offshore from Ninety Mile Beach. The fields developed here supply a fair proportion of the country's oil and natural gas requirements at present, but the future outlet is rather bleak if no more is found.

The pioneers of Gippsland are remembered with pride at the Moe Folk Museum which exhibits a collection of buildings and other items of interest associated with the early years. Another link with the past has been forged at the Coal Creek Historical Park at Korumburra which recreates a township built at the height of the coal mining boom days in South Gippsland. The busy town of Wonthaggi owes its existence to the black coal that was found there in 1909.

Gippsland's south-western extremity abuts onto the

A radiant sunset is reflected in the waters of Bass Strait at Cape Schanck on Victoria's southern coast.

sweeping shoreline of Westernport Bay which was discovered in 1798 by the explorer George Bass who described the surroundings as being 'low but hilly, the hills rising as they recede, which gives it a pleasing appearance.' A scatter of beach resorts cling to the margin of the bay and small farms dot the landscape beyond the shore. Phillip Island, which is one of Victoria's most popular holiday resorts, lies across the entrance to Westernport Bay. A bridge spanning the narrow Eastern Passage links San Remo on the mainland to Newhaven on the island.

Over the years, Phillip Island has been cleared of most of its natural vegetation but it still remains the home of a wide variety of indigenous wild-life. The favourites of the visitors are the tiny fairy penguins who raise their chicks in burrows among the sand dunes of Summerland Beach, returning after a day's fishing with food to feed their hungry families. They strut up the beach seeming to be quite unaware of the crowds who come to watch them. Phillip Island is also the breeding ground for all manner of sea birds, and a colony of koalas is also thriving. The Bass Strait fur seal population can be seen basking on Seal Rocks which lie off the Nobbies on the south-western side of the island. These seals were almost wiped out in the 19th Century when their skins were greatly in demand.

The McHaffie family, who arrived during the 1840s, were the island's first permanent settlers, although sealers working in Bass Strait had set up camp there for varying periods prior to that.

Victoria's first seeds were planted on nearby Churchill Island by Lieutenant James Grant in 1801, and Captain Samuel Wright landed at Rhyll in 1826 with the intention of forming a settlement. He later moved to Corinella on the mainland and the colony was finally abandoned in 1829. In summer, Phillip Island is crowded with visitors who enjoy all the activities it has to offer. Many have settled permanently in the new housing estates which have recently been developed.

Westernport Bay is separated from its neighbour Port Phillip by the Mornington Peninsula which is fringed along its length by beach resorts and suburbs within easy commuter reach of the city. The land beyond the coastal strip is sprinkled with small farms, orchards and market gardens, which are now being threatened by the spreading tentacles of the city. The Mornington Peninsula offers a wide variety of pleasant pastimes to Melbourne residents who can enjoy swimming or boating in the sheltered waters of the bay or surfing on the beaches fronting the wild waters of Bass Strait. The Cape Schanck Coastal Park, which encloses this portion of the

The picturesque Gippsland Lakes are popular with holiday-makers. The lively resort town of Lakes Entrance is located near the man-made entrance which was completed in 1889.

These hot pools at Metung in Gippsland are supplied by water from a bore drilled by the Port Addis Company while exploring for oil during the late 1920s.

The Yallourn power station in the Latrobe Valley is fuelled by brown coal laid down by prehistoric forests millions of years ago.

These lamps outside the Court House at Sale are lit with natural gas from the Bass Strait oil fields.

A whale's jawbones are a unique form of exterior decoration for the hotel at Wonthaggi, in south Gippsland.

Spreading trees shelter the ivy covered graves of four colonists who died during the brief life of Colonel Collin's settlement at Sorrento in 1803.

The Nobbies and Seal Rocks on the south-western side of Phillip Island. A colony of Bass Strait fur seals can often be seen basking on Seal Rocks. ➤

shoreline, contains some of the most spectacular scenery in the State. The coastline is very rugged and is ceaselessly pounded by the restless sea.

A monument on the beach at the popular resort of Sorrento in Port Phillip Bay marks the site of the first attempt to colonise the Port Phillip district in 1803. The settlers were under the command of Colonel David Collins who quickly became disenchanted with his choice of a site, saying that the soil was poor and the water supply inadequate. After four months the colony was abandoned and the settlers set sail for Tasmania. This was not an auspicious beginning to a story which was to be a continuing saga of outstanding and unqualified success. Shady trees in a small reserve shelter the ivy covered graves of four colonists who died during the settlement's brief life.

Victoria's chequered pattern of mountain ranges and forest, of small neat towns and large prosperous cities, of rivers winding through cool green valleys and a rugged coastline of rare and haunting beauty, remains long in the memory. There is, too, throughout the State an acute awareness of the part played by the early settlers who laid the cornerstone of its stability by their courage and fortitude. As well as building its economic strength, the pioneers, as they spread across the Colony created a multitude of gardens which today are woven into the landscape in a mosaic of living colour. From its foundation Victoria has been a blending of beauty and productivity and it is certain that as the 20th Century rushes to its close the Garden State will travel with it to the highest peaks of success.

*Tall masts and calm waters at the Newhaven Yacht Squadron
marina on Phillip Island.*

This bridge spanning the narrow Eastern Passage links San Remo on the mainland to Newhaven on Phillip Island.

Agnes Falls near Welshpool in Gippsland.